FACING YOUR FEAR OF DOGS

BY NICOLE A. MANSFIELD

PEBBLE
a capstone imprint

Published by Pebble, an imprint of Capstone
1710 Roe Crest Drive, North Mankato, Minnesota 56003
capstonepub.com

Library of Congress Cataloging-in-Publication Data is available on the Library of Congress website.
ISBN: 9780756574222 (hardcover)
ISBN: 9780756574055 (paperback)
ISBN: 9780756574185 (ebook PDF)

Summary: Describes the reasons for fearing dogs and simple tips to overcome these fears.

Editorial Credits
Editor: Erika L. Shores; Designer: Heidi Thompson; Media Researcher: Jo Miller; Production Specialist: Tori Abraham

Image Credits
Capstone Studio: Karon Dubke, 8, 9, 13; Getty Images: leventince, 17, mgstudyo, 5, Renee Pan / EyeEm, 6, SolStock, 4; Shutterstock: bubutu, 19, Domira, (background), cover and throughout, gpointstudio, Cover, 18, Kapitosh, (cloud), cover and throughout, Khamidulin Sergey, 15, l i g h t p o e t, 7, Marish, Marish (brave girl), cover and throughout, pogonici, 21, Volodymyr Plysiuk, 11

Printed and bound in China.   PO5377

TABLE OF CONTENTS

Words in **bold** are in the glossary.

SCARED OF DOGS

Dogs can be fun pets. But an excited jumping pup or a loud barking pooch might scare you. Many people have fears about dogs. Learning about dogs and knowing how to **interact** with them can help you feel calmer around them.

UNDERSTANDING DOGS

Do you remember a time you felt afraid of a dog? Did it chase you? Has a big dog growled or barked at you? Dogs **communicate** through the way they act and the sounds they make.

Did you know dogs "talk" with their tails? People use words, but dogs use wags! Dogs use their tails to tell us how they feel.

When a dog feels friendly, its body will be relaxed. A happy dog will keep its tail below the height of its back. It will loosely wag its tail. These are signs it wants to get to know you.

A slowly wagging tail is a sign of an unfriendly dog. This dog's body will be stiff. The dog is showing you it is not relaxed.

A high tail, whether wagging or still, means a dog is on alert. It may feel **threatened**. It might growl and become **aggressive** if you get closer.

STAYING SAFE AROUND DOGS

Being approached by a dog can be scary. It's normal to want to run away. But running or shouting can make things worse. Dogs like to play chase. An excited dog may run after you. It thinks you are playing.

If the sight of a dog scares you, take a few deep breaths. Do not run. Stand very still. Stay stiff with your arms by your side. Look down at the ground. Don't stare the dog in the eyes. By staying still and calm, the dog will lose interest in you. It will leave you alone.

FACING YOUR FEAR

One day you may want to learn how to make friends with a dog. Always ask a dog's owner if it is safe to pet their dog. If the owner says yes, then you can decide if you want to get closer. Allowing the dog to sniff you is how you introduce yourself.

Look for signs that the dog is relaxed. Is its tail low and wagging? You might hold out your hand. The dog will sniff it and maybe even lick you. You might decide to pet the dog on its neck or shoulders.

You may never love dogs. But you can learn to face your fears. You can be brave around dogs.

STAY STILL HIDE-AND-SEEK

You can send a message to a dog that you don't want to play by staying stiff and still. With nothing moving, a dog will get bored and go away. Here's a hide-and-seek game you can play with friends to practice your dog safety skills.

What You Need

- At least two friends
- A stuffed toy dog or other stuffed animal

What You Do

1. Close your eyes. Have a friend hide a stuffed toy dog or other stuffed animal.

2. When your friend is ready, you and your other friend search for the stuffed animal.

3. When you and your friend find the toy, you must follow dog safety rules:
    - Do not touch the toy.
    - Stand still and stay stiff.
    - Put your arms down by your side and stare at the ground.

4. Your friend who hid the toy will start counting. The winner is the person who stays still and quiet the longest. Then the winner takes a turn at hiding the toy.

GLOSSARY

aggressive (uh-GREH-siv)—strong and forceful; ready to attack

communicate (kuh-MYOO-nuh-kate)—to make information known to another

interact (in-tur-AKT)—to have action with others

threatened (THRET-uhnd)—expressing an aim or possibility to do harm

READ MORE

Hamilton, Kersten. *What's Up, Pup?: How Our Furry Friends Communicate and What They Are Saying.* New York: Farrar Straus Giroux Books for Young Readers, 2022.

Kidd, Gideon and Braunigan, Rachel. *Pet That Dog! A Handbook for Making Four-Legged Friends.* Philadelphia: Quirk Books, 2020.

Mattern, Joanne. *Dogs.* Minneapolis: Bellwether Media, 2021.

INTERNET SITES

Dogs You Know: Be Safe
youtube.com/watch?v=JZGOEYkfVwE

Learn to Speak Dog
doggonesafe.com/Learn-to-Speak-Dog-Campaign

INDEX

ABOUT THE AUTHOR

Nicole A. Mansfield is a wife, mother and educator. She dedicates this book to the people who have taught her the most, her family—Connie, Walter, and Cheryl Mills, Justin, Victorious, Justine, and Zion Mansfield. Nicole is passionate about serving at her church and vacationing at the beach!